doc.x

JOANNE GODLEY

Published by Black Sunflowers Poetry Press
www.blacksunflowerspoetry.com

© Joanne Godley 2024

ISBN: 978-1-7396267-6-1

All rights reserved.

These poems are dedicated to the memory of my mother, Juanita Fitzpatrick Godley, a medical professional and social justice advocate in her own right, who, from the onset of my lengthy medical training and career, repeatedly urged me to write, write, write. And to my sister-doctors, we contain multitudes.

What they call you is one thing.
   What you answer to is something else.

—Lucille Clifton

TABLE OF CONTENTS

The Hospital	1
Platitudes from an Old Fart	4
Two Blackfruit Trees perish Daily Producing Fruit	5
The next magic trick	6
A Black Lab Tech at Johns Hopkins Medical School, Receives Post-mortem Honorary Medical Degree	8
Bare	9
each time, first time	10
but, where?	12
The real sister doctors of mercy wear house calls	14
untitled	15
A person with a Medical Doctorate	16
Indiana Jones Completes the Job	17
Squeamish	19
Is There a Doctor in the House?	21
Dear Clarice	22
Acknowledgements	25

The Hospital

Come, doctor at Mercy hospital.

This westerly blemish on brotherly love.
Hallways dim-lit.
Self-pay patients shackled to beds.
Yellowed walls bleached by screams.
Wards stacked four flimsy-curtained beds deep.

This wear-house of community stats:
of babies born too soon and small,
of mother's paths 'unfore-nothing-we-could-do-seen',
of late-stage cancers,
of those perceived to have hardly-never pain,
of pressures high and higher
of 5-year mortalities equaling zero,
of body 'thickness' and 'sugar' seasonal as sun,
of mental illnesses floridly unseen,
of paranoia, a survival necessity.

See us, there, starched in white doctor-coats,
eager to cure.
Some, with nowhere else to practice.
some, do-goodism-drenched. We jostle
to shoulder Atlas's load.

Here nurses scurry like worker ants,
tireless,
team-focused,
tenacious.
In the patient's service:
they bathe, they scold, they medicate, they feed, they bandage,
they commiserate,
they defend.

And the nuns, of course,
blanched-holy, placid,

full of deter-me-not grace, murmured
years fade white to Black.
Like sturdy elms shielding this red brick-faced building,
an edifice scaffolded by prayers.

Doctors bolster hospital's reputation,
even as neighbors try to steer clear:
"Take me there—-only if my soul's lost its will."
"——Only if my blood runs thick rivulets in the street,
past the corner church;"
"——-Only if I'm shot real bad, near death,
and the rest of city's hospitals have closed.
Otherwise, if I'm breathing, take me elsewhere."

Misery hospital hallowed be thy name.

    2-

Smells?
Yes, smells. Betadine, old blood, piss, poop, Clorox, alcohol of the isopropyl type, hurried sex, transitioning souls.

What colors?
Colors swirl in endless curlicues: try grieving greige, prejudicial puce, fearful framboise, compassionate carmine.

What sounds?
Sounds abound. The untethered wail of a newborn, the stricken wail of a newly sonless mother, the sorrowful wail of an off-duty nurse revisiting, the muffled wail of an on-call doctor pleasured.

What is felt:
grief shrouded as spousal despair,
the flinch of venipunctured bodies,
the jolt of an ancient elevator,
curated pain, courtesy of a stingy anesthetist.

-3-

We, Black, professional.
We, Black beleaguered soldiers,
medical school a battleground
of coveted knowledge cordoned
in enemy terrain.
Our mission,
secure bounty with essence intact.
In war of attrition, we, sisters survived.
Black like our patients, who, mainly are proud,
like our aunties and mothers, who sacrificed much,
like our beaten fathers, neighbors, and friends,
all watching us step onto tumultuous waters,
all expecting us to sink tall.
We, Black women, not vixens nor mammies,
nor superwomen-Saras
with flowing red capes.
We bleed when cut,
we harbor dreams and have flaws.
Entertainers not, we need not smile on cue.

We, the real sisters of mercy.

Platitudes from an Old Fart

Let me curbside you--
I have been medicinal
on this hairy borborygmi
for a hiatus—un-herniated.
life is— if you know how—
wildly gastrointestinal!
tenesmus, torsion, bilirubin, belch!
try not to be too acid—
dysentery can and will be yours
savor the ischemia; it digests the flatulent polyps
never ever ulcer a woman—
it causes dysentery, chyme and does not work
splenic your tidings and liver it up
the antacid way dulls the viscera
spread your esophagus far and wide,
mesenteric around, until—
intussusception is yours to bloat, my bile.

Two Blackfruit Trees Perish Daily Producing Fruit

For more than three decades in the Yellow Hammer state,
Margaret Charles Smith, a young sharecropper,
tended blackfruit trees. She out-produced others
anointed to this work, though the soil was meager and her seedlings
frail, and elemental Southern treachery sought to smite them all.
Her tree survival stats were chalked up to sorcery and fate

*What did she know? What did she
know about the marriage of love and gardening?*

The Black Mamas Matter Alliance, in fits of retrospective despair,
sought the secrets to Miss Margaret's blackfruit tree survival.
Sought to drown the sick sound of desecrated limbs,
sought to tamp the odor of dead bark decay (that tears at the heart,
and crumbles the gut). Not to mention that
the ground-littered festering of orphaned fruit
so angered the ancestors. The erasure of blackfruit tree presence wept the
notes to a silenced song

*What did she know? What did she
know about the marriage of love and gardening?*

Few understand soil and tree sentience,
that the soil yearned constantly for Miss Margaret's gentling,
that the trees lifted and stretched when she stroked them and sang
in tree-language of trust. Few understand
that preservation of mother-life requires heartfelt assurance
that blackfruit trees are vital to this world

*What did she know? What did she
know about the marriage of love and gardening?*

the next magic trick

newsflash: Black women in America are a well-cared for sector of the U.S. population, especially, during childbirth

extended family members cease hugging James, re-wrap the baby gifts they'd brought, and leave the hospital

        James' tears slide into-his tear ducts

James hands his swaddled newborn daughter to the nurses, their faces upcast instead of down

        they un-swaddle the infant who begins to scream

the doctor eases the baby into your waiting womb

        your heart monitor begins a steady *beep-beep*

dark blood splattered about the OR table, walls, ceiling, floors, and staff gowns, grows lighter in color, coalesces, and seeps into your body

        the doctor's shouts return to his throat

the nurses' expressions are placid, their movements no longer frantic,

        the anaesthesiologist withdraws medicine through a syringe from your arm, rouses you,

and terror leaves your body

        your husband smiles as you return to the birthing suite

blood covering the floor and bed re-enter your system

        you swallow your screams

pieces of white plaster fly from floor to wall, cover the imprint of James's fist

                the open wound across his knuckles disappears as he resorbs his fury

the two of you, pregnant with hope, leave the hospital

                rain droplets ascend like chariots into the kingdom sky

A Black Lab Tech at Johns Hopkins Medical School, Receives Postmortem Honorary Medical Degree

— for Vivien Theodore Thomas

"I set the test tubes aside
Doc needed a hand with the retractors

they told me. So, I scrubbed in like
he'd taught me and stood by his side.

Out of the spotlight glare.
Looked down at the blood pool, made out

those tubes like tiny webs yawning out from the baby's heart.
Heard the beep beep music of the monitor.

Waited to let him know I's there, quiet
and low, so's *not* to catch him off-guard,

tremble his hand and mistake the patient.
Soon realized Doc had it backwards. I placed

my gloved hand over his, moved it toward
the right heart vessels. "You wanna clamp

this one, not that." Showed him again later
when the surgery was over, the patient recovering

nicely. We practice the same surgery
on the dogs, over and over, 'til he gets it right.

Heart surgery's not easy unless you
do it a bunch, like me, on the dogs in the lab."

Bare

When you called us 'essential' workers
I embraced it with doctorly grace.
when we were dismissed as 'dispensable,' I balked.
When it became clear nurses and doctors would not
be shielded against the inferno,
I handed in my weatherworn stethoscope.
No amount of clapping could make me fly
naked into this storm

each time, first time

wash and glove hands,
breath
take scope in hand, as a violinist cradles an ancient Stradivari,
caress her with reverence. she that allows you to see.
the black-headed five-foot instrument, coiled, gleams like a patient snake.
how the head hugs the palm like a guitar-fingers free to access varied-colored buttons
tap air/ water button hear swoosh-release of air; see swift pulse water.
place snake tip in water basin,
watch as she slurps water into inner chamber.
flick on scope light.
music by Buika begins—in deep, reverent tones.
dim lights.
turn to patient, now in dreamland, thanks to Diprovan's magic,
breath deep.
lubricate scope's tip, she that shares her view.
glide into patient's open mouth.
each intubation, each procedure, each time I am permitted to explore the inner sanctuary of another being, I am humbled.
push scope forward, slick mucous in the mouth eases scope's passage into food tube then to the stomach, empty by design
seek a child's mind.
keep knowledge and expectations in rear-view.
be a seeker draped in awe. inside this holy gustatory tube. inside, we are all glistening salmon pink.
valve to stomach opens, a vacuous blush-pink cave. undulates a *welcome, enter.*
because fiber optics and because of screen immensity, I am fully in my patient's belly.
Wow! Wow!
stomach walls, shining smooth. acid flows to greet food through lumpy bumpy channels along the floor. where the vessels run. stomach-cave narrows down to small hole, like a troll's mouth it opens and closes.
stomach's labor will begin:
will pulverize food, twisting, turning, kneading.

cavity will fill with bubbles of air, to make food-paste.
push paste towards troll-hole, that guards the small intestine's entrance, there
where nutrients are extracted with care.
bow to the body's second brain.
strange writhing world, silent system,
marvelous food processor,
the intestines,
unveiled by this scope, allows me to witness.
each time, first time

but, where?

Asks the patient of the Doctor
whose sunshine-seeking skin suggests more comfort in a bikini
collecting seashells
than an LLB flannel shirt   collecting firewood

Someone   Come   Recount Doc's maternal legacy
pelvic-housed gems passed like batons through women-generations
her great-grandmother's great grandmother's

Praise-be Place? What Place?
whose Middle Passenger relative determined neither to jump (ship)
nor be thrown to tag-along sharks &   must miss   dysentery TB syphilis
pregnancy   dehydration malnutrition & ship mutinies   to protect ovum

Sing endurance-praises to Doc's kin-group
wretched plantation hangings   cat o' nine tail whippings
            surviving breeding-farm rapes

Sing Praise Song for traumatized kindred
souls fed violence   with no rest-save death
 (*was that trauma passed down too?)*

Praise wombed-seedlings
planted in hostile terrain

Stand   Sing for Doc's Southern mother
who clutched tailwinds of Northerly migration
birthed a daughter   while wrestling   her version of the American Dream

Praise Song   For this path
the daughter finished Yale Med
Doc began a practice   that brought her to Maine
where this patient has failed to drink all the bowel prep
& the nurses and techs say—*we want to go home*

Praise Doc's procedure and diagnosis
emergency surgery for the cure

Praise Song for the patient's children
who, despite her cancer   will have the gift of seeing
their mother grow old

Yes , but where are you from-from Doc?

From-from? Who gives a good damn <u>where</u> the Doctor's from?

the real sister doctors of mercy wear house calls

> *–after 'the Cambridge ladies who live in furnished souls'*
> *— e. e. cummings*

the real sisters of mercy not reality tv but real.
because Philly doctors black and sister. not kin.
practices (also, mercy hospital, uncaring
uncharitable catholic-because) better than UPenn even
or suburbs they believe in evidence based diagnostic cash–
the real sister doctors of mercy wear house calls . . .
this is all history if. support a sister.
offer tasty medicine, am. Serious which doctor
is sleeping with which. perhaps. Home of cheese steak
and morbid obesity begets money.
sisterly affection is what gets you, brothers.
If anything, MOVE people. the mountain-laurel signifies
state. does that help codified pain?
Ms. Anderson? Mr. Coltrane? Mr. Robeson?
the heavens your tears whisper.

Where did you go to medical school?	Have you ever performed this procedure before?	What country are you from dear?	Your hair is so interesting! May I touch it?	You're so pretty! If my son brought you home, I wouldn't be made at all!
The entire office is afraid of you.	Where did you go to medical school?	You're different from other black people	Your parents must be proud of you!	Google agrees your medical advice is correct!
You speak so well! So articulate!	Would you make sure my room gets clean towels?	You should smile more!	My housekeeper has the same last name as yours. Do you know her?	When I spoke with you on the phone, I had no idea...
You're the doctor? The hell no!	How ever did you find the money to go to medical school?	Is that your son? I bet he played basketball in high school, right?	Where did you go to medical school?	That patient complained that he felt inferior around you
Where did you go to medical school?	You really seem to know what you're doing...	Do you have some proof that you're the doctor?	Now that you're here, would you make sure that my trash is emptied?	I'll wait. I prefer to be seen by the doctor.

A PERSON WITH A MEDICAL DOCTORATE

-after "A Position at the University" by Lydia Davis

Knowing myself as I do, I admit that I would not be the type of person I might envision as having a medical doctorate from Yale. But since I do have a medical doctorate and it is from Yale, I must be the sort of person who holds a medical doctorate from Yale. This should provide comfort to me, on the off-chance I were to be stopped by the police for a traffic issue, or if the police were to enter my home to check the premises in case I mistakenly left the door ajar, or if the police were summoned because I complained, albeit vigorously, to a store manager over a customer service issue that irritated me, and the police might try to presume what type of person I am.

But supposing I am not wearing a recently starched and pressed white coat with my name embroidered in maroon thread over the right breast pocket and a Littman stethoscope draped casually around my neck? Even then, ninety percent of the time, I am asked, "Oh, from what medical school did you matriculate?" This, even though any clinic or hospital in which I work will have thoroughly credentialed all their physicians to verify our respective backgrounds and licenses as well as our medical doctorates and even though I finished medical school more than 40 years ago and have the grey hair to prove it. It is unclear whether the police would have the wherewithal or knowledge to glean the numbers of times I comforted people in their time of medical need or the number of times I prevented or diagnosed cancer in individuals whom an officer might even know.

Knowing that I am often accused by professional colleagues of not speaking loudly enough in group settings, I would push my greying locks away from my face and say, in an authoritative voice to the officers summoned over whatever niggling issue, "I have a medical doctorate." I would say this holding my Yale medical school degree against my chest, all the while cognizant of the fact that a wood-framed sheet of sheepskin with Latin inscription offers little protection against thirsty, black-body-seeking bullets.

Indiana Jones Completes the Job

I happened upon an IJ movie
my kids were watching
with mouths-wide-open.
Did his quest make my stomach do a flip?
Did the climax make my muscles go limp?
Did his antics cause arm goosebumps to rise to attention?
Yes, yes, and yes.

I closed my eyes later that night unaware a spell
was cast—was paged back to the hospital- amidst my dream.
There was a man—with bloody vomitus plagued by stomach ulcers in the past.
Would I seek the cause of the bleeding,
and resolve it straightaway?

To seek the dragon inside, to find the dragon spewing blood, to find the dragon
spewing blood and slay it.

Slick and wet and slick and dark, one enters this, like any mouth—
with consent.

This cavernous cave, salaciously pink— this tongue—
ride this tongue, as you slide
your scope back—while this tongue writhes you back, writhes you back—
(now stay the course).
Then a muscular door bids you pass—into a tunnel—darker pink-another trek.

Who has never longed
to don the life of one so fortunate
as to journey in the Amazon,
seeking herbal magic cures?

Or be an explorer on a hero's
journey with arctic discoveries
a la Henson?

Slog through pools
of dark blood—puddled
in the stomach's base.
A crimson haze clouds
your vision-path.
So, you suction with speed
on the hunt for the source
of this offensive spew,
to turn off the offending spigot.

You snake 'round a corner—
There, a craggy crater looms.
In the center, like an island, a grey nubbin,
that, like a geyser, spurts—
pulsing blood to a '1-2' beat.

 Arrange your armaments
of choice: choose a tool
that, like a clothespin,
chokes the vessel off—
clips its wings—
so, to speak—a clip
that dams back the blood—
stops the surge-like a burp
held back.

You back out while surveilling
this landscape that you know—
with its pink hills and cobbled valleys
(Where acid's known to secrete)
this place made of glistening writhing muscle,
This foray into intestines,
days you're honored
to seek and slay blood dragons.

Squeamish

1

an empty bed in the ICU
calls you for a few hours of sleep
quicker than you can say 'boo'
you've laid down and gone fast asleep

—wakened minutes later from a deep dream
nurse says bed # 2's 'sundowning' again
(*couldn't she wake another doctor on the team?*
why not one of the men?)

being an intern means you handle all scut
witness the drumbeat of a 'gone-rogue' artery
watch tar-poop scurry out a patient's gut
and skirt another's feral mockery

you recall that black poop means blood
best keep drinking coffee 'cuz there's no meal in sight
tiredness embraces you like an old bud
all day working and into the night

2

leave rounds to go pray in the chapel
recall gurgles heard through the stethoscope
a doc sneezes reaching for the scalpel
old blood in the belly looks like black strands of rope

dying strangers to whom you offer comfort
then you flee to the bathroom for a good cry
blinking tears because a patients' days are numbered
bleary-red, dog-tired eyes

you admonish the younger docs to 'please do no harm'
while a ward clerk's radio is tuned to Motown
someone's heart-beat problems trigger an alarm
a random nurse quietly breaks down

sickly odor of *fetor hepaticus*
constant beep of monitors   buzzing of pagers
surgeon colleague tries to land kisses
colleague's on-call room sonorous behaviors

you tremble   not to come undone
in the background a repetitive *boom–beep-beep*
the hospital backlit by the setting-sun's swoon
what you really need, doctor, is good sleep

Is There a Doctor in the House?

Delirious with pain and with little money, the young physician went to see a doctor.
She burst into tears when the clinic told her the visit was courtesy and free for doctors.

A wine connoisseur adored everything about the grape but failed to pass the sommelier exam.
When he finally passed the sommelier test, his friends anointed him, The Chablis Doctor.

Before medical ethics was birthed, physicians were looked up to like virtual Gods.
Back then, no patient would ever have had the temerity to disagree with a doctor.

That nerdy PHD student studying climate change and pesticides,
found out he'd acquired the dreaded nickname of the 'DDT doctor.'

She had begun to lose her sight until a radical surgical intervention restored it—
In honor of this miraculous event, she declared eye surgeons be called 'sight-see doctors.'

We are fearless in our willingness to explore parts of the body other folks would rather not go.
This poet suggests that gastroenterologists be acknowledged as the 'gutsy doctors.'

Dear Clarice,

You know that sprig of spiked-leaf greenery, mistletoe, people kiss under during the holidays? It's parasitic. In the wild, it attaches to the vascular system of other trees or shrubs and slowly destroys them by sucking away at their life-giving essences.

The medical care system attaches itself to the altruism of physicians and nurses. It asks you to give and give and give some more. As a doctor, you are hard-wired to say 'yes.' You give to patients, to insurance companies (all those hours on the phone arguing about a test or a drug you know the patient needs), to bevies of nurses who just want you to look at the patient in room #3, to hospital administrators, to the electronic medical record seemingly designed to frustrate (for billing purposes) and, to, really, whoever asks. You are sucked dry.

I fear for you, Clarice. I fear for us.

*****

I don't recall the year you reach out to me. At the time, my brother is doing his medicine residency.

He calls one day and asks, "Sis, remember Clarice? From my med school class?"

And, I say, "Sure, I remember her!"

Who can forget you? Beautiful and bright-eyed. You and he are so much alike– a keen sense of wit, infectious laugh, and fierce intellect. I remind my brother about something silly you did or said back when we were all in Boston together and we both explode with laughter over the phone.

After a pause, he says, "Hey, can she call you? Things are a little rough for her in her surgical residency and she'd like to speak with you."

But of course.

Before signing off, he slips in the small detail about your suicide attempt and how your training program supervisor advised you to take a week off before returning to the hospital. Maybe, they put you on antidepressants. Maybe, he doesn't say. I am sure he says you are in counseling. Or are being referred for it. I am dismayed and saddened for you. At the time, I am juggling mothering a newborn, with being newly married, with coming to grips with my husband's covert alcoholism, with working as an ER attending at the U of P, all while grieving my mother's protracted demise from metastatic colon cancer several states away. Nonetheless, I wait to hear from you.

*****

You do call and you sound exactly like the Clarice I know. *The old Clarice.* Not suicidal, not depressed. You don't ponder the wisdom of having chosen medicine as a career nor do you question the fact that you chose the *bad ass* of specialties, surgery, which allows no time for yourself. You do not complain about anything. You do not mention how grueling the training is, nor how demeaning, nor that there are no mentors for smart, brown-skinned women who want to become proficient surgeons, nor that your colleagues are not collegial, nor even civil, that you are the only woman, that there is no place for you to change into your scrubs. You fail to mention that you have not seen your family in a while despite the fact they are in Brooklyn, one borough over. You do not mention your weight loss. You do not reveal that you have become an expert retractor-holder. Nor did you drop the fact that you have not, in your year of surgical residency, performed any surgery. Nor do you bring up the prowess with which you can now fetch coffee, or a stethoscope left on an attending's desk, nor how effortless it has become to not laugh at the barrage of slurs slung about in your presence. None of that. You share a bit. I share a bit. We keep it light. You keep trying to make ME laugh. Not once do I try to be your doctor. I listen like the friend I imagine you have no time to cultivate. I do not talk about things I do not yet know:

1) That, a silent epidemic of physician suicides is brewing---ever since insurance companies began to insert themselves between physicians and patients.

2) That, on average, at least, one physician commits suicide every day.
3) That, Black women are at highest risk for suicide in the U.S.
4) That, for an empath like you, the corporatization of medicine risks causing you *moral injury.*

A few years pass until, out of the blue, my brother calls and informs me that you ended it all. And, that you had been attempting to do so, for many years. He is devastated. I am distraught. Why did I not keep up with you? Talk with you more? Speak to you with more intimacy? Why did I not probe your issues? Warn you?   Shield you? Express my concern and care?

How

    could I have

        saved you?

           saved you?

              saved you?

Acknowledgements

A Person with a Medical Document was first published in *Bellevue Literary Review*, Issue 40, 2021.

www.blacksunflowerspoetry.com

www.ingramcontent.com/pod-product-compliance
Lightning Source LLC
Chambersburg PA
CBHW040639100526
44585CB00039B/2870